collecting ..￼u￼er where we will

Collette Sell's poems are beautiful, evocative prayers, each immediate, inspiring, and intimate, brimming with surprising images. There are 52, but you won't want to space them out one week at a time: you'll want to devour them—and then, hungry for more, start all over again. I loved them.

~Paola Gianturco, author, photographer

How can we not cry *Take me with you!* to Collette Sell for these beautiful, generous, dangerous, infinitely tender poems? These love songs to a timeless present, sing with longing, wit, delight, and fire.

~Ruth Kirschner, playwright, poet

Collette Sell's brilliant new collection is like nothing you've ever read. These poems/prayers shimmer with vivid imagery, spiritual wisdom, and deeply felt experiences of gratitude, supplication, sorrow, and delight. They rejoice in the beauty of the natural world and rage against the injustice that humans create. Finally, they invite us into the essential human work of wonder.

~Alexander Levering Kern, poet, editor of
Pensive: A Global Journal of Spirituality & the Arts

Collecting Wonder Where We Will is a book of exploration, questions, desires. The poet is on a journey and encourages the reader to come along. Full of wonderful and original images, we appreciate what has been given to us, and ways of participating, paying attention to the lovely as well as the coming darkness. There is life and there is death and there is the journey in between of discovery and acceptance. The title alone is an invitation from the poet to the reader. This is a book to contemplate long after you have closed the cover.

~CB Follett, Poet Laureate Emerita of Marin County, California

In this honest reckoning of self to soul, *Collecting Wonder Where We Will,* Collette Sell shares invocations and insights that emerge from our collective human longing: "Give me a day of Yes... Praise Death's Forgiveness... Lay the reunion feast." Early on in this, her first collection, the poet confesses, "I cannot tell you if I'm lazy or wise." But as we venture with her "past the known," we witness the growth of her kinship (& ours) with grasshopper and snake, and "what is wild in the brambles." By the last pages, "tingling with time" we enter a lighter sense of being -- capable of "tightrope-walking the thin light under the door."

~Prartho Sereno, Poet Laureate Emerita of
Marin County, California, founder of
*The Poetic Pilgrimage: Poem-Making
as Spiritual Practice,*

Collette Sell's poems read like stunning incantations. Raw, vulnerable moments and heart-lifting revelations are spun together in a tapestry of gorgeous, sensual prosody. *Collecting Wonder* has a sense of timelessness—prayers to the sun, the moon, the goddesses, and the ancestors—poems honoring the urgency of the country's need for change and social justice. The narrative of the writer's personal struggles arrives in sharp, honest stabs. Yet the poet's journey is deeply interlaced with the natural world just outside her door. The lines reverberate with universal human experiences—guilt, pain and frustration, deep love and grief, hope and healing. In riveting stanzas that pulse with longing, awareness and even humor, the poet's strong voice emerges through faith in something—in the natural world's bounty, in the change-makers who came before, in the cool blue smoke of gratitude. Readers will find themselves reading the poems over and over, and each time finding a new moment of connection.

~ Joanell Serra, poet, author of
*(Her)oics: Women's Lived Experiences
During the Coronavirus Pandemic*

collecting wonder where we will

collecting wonder where we will

collette sell

Wild Rising Press

EVERGREEN, COLORADO

Cover Illustration: Terry Hertz, San Miguel de Allende, Mexico
Editor: Judyth Hill
Book & Cover Design: Mary M. Meade
Torn paper: starline on Freepik.com

www.wildrisingpress
ISBN 978-1-957468-07-5—First Edition

...here is the deepest secret nobody knows
(here is the root of the root and the bud of the bud
and the sky of the sky of a tree called life; which grows
higher than soul can hope or mind can hide)
and this is the wonder that's keeping the stars apart...

—E.E. CUMMINGS

AN INVITATION FROM THE AUTHOR

These poems sprang to life as prayers, not to a specific deity, but to spirits greater than our own. I invite you to read them with that in mind. However, if words like "prayer," "holy," and "sacred" are not meaningful to you, please let these poems find a place in your heart.

1

Goddess One, Two, Three, Four, One Thousand
in all the pantheons of all the ages—
see me as your own, born of sorrow and joy,
deep—wide, high—low, over—under, light—dark.

Every duality at once.

Let all these opposites come together,
a great shimmer of petals that fall
upon my shoulders.

Make me know myself as your own.

2

I scold my nose for keeping on the grindstone.
My fingers for scratching the surface.
My stitches desperate to bind time.

Lift me instead to Majesty so large
I have to shut my eyes to see it.

Gather the skirts of wet skies,
sweep hems across acres of roses.

Show me the heavens under eyelids,
mountains too small for the Holy.

Lose me to glory, not mine, but yours,
so I might live there without edges.

3

Even with shutters, the light enters,
slides past wood and metal and glass
to find me here.

Ah, I invite you—set fire to me.
Allow me to be consumed,
I have been waiting so long.

Blaze me with heat.
Send lightning down my spine
to where desire lives.

Ignite flames of longing
in the braids of my hair.
I will lie so still.

4

I used to think that prayers
went straight to heaven,
that all things upright—
steeples, redwood trees, blades of grass—
sent prayers upward from our fear.
Sun and moon showered
down their grace in answer.

It has taken my long life,
till today—to understand:
prayers are everywhere,
murmurations above cascading water.

Over jagged ravines
they tie knotted handholds
for our long-awaited transit.

If we stretch, we'll catch the net,
and sway above the rocks.
Prayers and blessings crisscross,
a bridge across time,
a cradle for all the days
we still hope to share.

5

Teach me the weight of apple blossoms.
Petals like white butterflies
land in my dark hair.
Gravity did this.

Guide my steps on sun-warmed stones,
inside the open gate.
Tell my feet I am home.
Sunlight did this.

Call wild ducks,
reflected from the sky on
sequined ripples of evening.
Breezes did this.

Remind me again today
that this tender light
connects me
to Goodness everywhere.

6

This is what I need to hear:
It is not impossible.

Holy Mothers' songs
spin the double mysteries
of birth and death,
how one becomes the other
while the black holes
suck us through their teeth.

This is what I need to hear,
There is nothing to forgive.
Choose your own atonement.

Candles light themselves
from stars that have no eyes
but still intend to glow.
Smoke trails upward,
pulls the tail of fear
out the window.

This is what I need to hear,
Change your skin,
even if you have to crawl.

Oil poured from a jade pitcher
slips off my skin.
A snake thinks I am kin
to lowly things or beings
almost underfoot. But

even snakes can climb
to wind themselves in trees.

This is what I need to hear.
You have hands to clear
the angry mouths of screams.

Knit lullabies from rage.
Twist the wool of sorrow
over painted birchwood spindles
for the mighty Legend Women
who weave tomorrow's rivers.

All the Impossibles will be set to rights.
Gather their heartbeats,
sweep up their footsteps.
Pack up their curses
in spiny rucksacks to bury under pines
gleaming with cables of silk,
bridges made by spiders
who believe nothing is impossible.

7

Raise my hands,
and lift my heart
in praise of pomegranates.

A bowl of scarlet pips
curled in creamy halos
on the sideboard of my sink.

Crimson seeds stain my fingers,
a communion of possibility.
We need not pick and choose—

but gently slide the silky seeds
from moonglow nests, then
swallow whole their blessings.

8

Only with Spring
might you answer the rockslide
approaching your bed. Come:
hope to rise you up like
wind against the stone;
breath blowing blossoms amber, ruby, violet,
scratching at the glass of death.

Lie with me and listen
for the fall of boulders spilling
down beside our meadow.
We are saved by blossoms every day.

9

It is not enough to open up, you say,
but seek out where the Goddess lives,
curled in acorns, awaiting flames.

It is not enough to see the Goddess.
You must brush her lips with rosemary.
Let her swallow you.

It is not enough to feel
the smooth breath of evening.
Let her share her breath with you.

It is not enough to stay here
in the skin you already know
in the comfort of lullabies.

Venture past the Named.

Arrive Nameless.

10

Fill me with light.
Make me glow like the lantern
in a forest hut, radiant,
giving myself away.

They say I must
save some for myself,
squirrel away oil and flame
to chase my own shadows.

Worry, they say, hold on
to all the bits, to shards of mirror,
lightning bolts, setting suns,
you will need them all.

I cannot tell you if I am lazy
or wise, lying here,
shining on, saving nothing.
But I am glad of it.

11

I do not understand Time.
Or Place. Or Destiny. Or Stars.
Or Light. Or Love.
Or anything but Gravity.

Force pulls feet into mud,
humbles flight, calls lemons
to leap from the tree
while I climb for a better look.

I could be a Seeker,
lifting one bare foot.
Toes feel for the path
of insects over mountains.

Gravity surrenders to the fall,
drops us where we land
side-by-side, surprised by skin,
by not much more than bones.

We could ask for Grace,
rise together,
walk and rest and pray.

I'm tired of praying for myself.
I will pray for you.

12

May Heaven give us more words
for hill paths, mountain tracks, desert roads.
We know the landscape with our feet,
but search for meaning on the trail.

Help me begin again to climb
relentless rise of naked hills
carrying this pack of darkness
longer, higher.

Help me greet the seekers on the road,
to offer aid and comfort,
water, apples, soft cloth
for aching feet.

Help me hold up the travelers
who lean against the rocks,
along edges strewn with weeds,
exhausted by vows.

Help me bathe their faces,
eyes closed to all but faith,
the destiny they seek
on hills too far to know.

Let go the measure of the road,
the counting of the pilgrim steps.
Speak new words to me:
devotion, endurance, love.

Those virtues I did not set out to find.

13

Please teach me to stop;
I am tired of running.

Please teach me rest;
I am tired of planning.

Please teach me quiet;
I am tired of yelling.

Please teach me peace;
I am tired of protesting.

Please help me call back my vows
to shelter humanity,
to protect the children,
to honor the mothers,
to save the earth.

Give me strength
to search the eyes
and take the hands
of one more generation.

I will carry their water.
They can stand on my shoulders.
I offer homemade signs, my megaphone
still ready after seventy-one years of war.

Only now, when I am old,
I see there is no end.

Nor, my friends,
is there an end to Good.

14

Let me lose things.
Don't pick them up
as you sidle along behind.

Let them fall from my fingers.
My shoulders. My mouth.
To drop through time.

Let them lie petaled in the street,
marigolds on cobblestones
to help the Dead find Home.

Let me call The Lost by name—
Patrick and Joe, Greg, Terry,
Tom and Pete, dear Burke, Alice and Luis.

Let them walk with me
beside a hundred unmarked graves,
lay white lilies on their breasts.

Welcome my lost friends,
lay the reunion feast, light the midnight candles
before morning empties our arms, again.

15

White skin stretching over hills
bleached by sun, dry golden dust
not pausing for this prayer.

Specks winking overhead
wait for the moon to make them stars,
then stardust falls on hills again
and sends us back to song.

Pray for water, pray for moon,
for shadows, not for night.
Tides spin back, dissolve the dunes,
the horizon disappears.

We pray together in the dark,
bodies bare of comfort, only
feathers in a heap,
just enough to clothe us.

Water calls to sand,
sand calls back to water.
Make me something you can use
before the tide returns.

16

Bring me to my knees
where the violet trumpet vine
winds through cactus,
the weight of olives arches overhead.
The sky sucks water from the well,
leaves behind the dust of haste.

A grasshopper not yet
baptized by the rain,
searches for grass forests.
I sing to him
of thickets inside skin,
the tangle membranes make.

In some other darkness
we converse of pruning limbs
as water cracks the well.
Old Iron reveals the blacksmith's forge.
Heat summons the scent of limes
through terracotta squares.

Let these words be an offering.
I hold cupped hands to Heaven.

17

Who can be grateful
for the teachings of pain?
Messiness of tears,
blood of the next cut?

Every cell yearns to stop
in my desperate tracks.
Rock me to dreams or death.
Either will do.

Do you know how long
light will shine under my skin?
It's not so sure, you know,
that, cursed, I will resist the end.

Will it come when I have had enough?
Enough scalding showers to defy my pain.
Enough sad movies to purge my tears.
Enough past to see nothing ahead.

I shut the door to chatter.
Close curtains to the street.
Wonder which pleasures
will be worth more days.
Which promises, more nights.

18

I thought I could make heat.

Cold swallows me.
Inside the whale of ice,
I touch the cavern walls.

I make no heat.
My eyes freeze shut.
I cannot lift them up to pray.

Still I remember how to chant
with icebound lips,
a psalm for dying.

Ardent arctic mouth
begs communion,
one scarlet berry,
from a bunting beak.

Whispering the Sanctus
I surrender my bones to fire.

19

I could scream red curses
from the roof
lean against a steeple
washing cities with my tears.

I could rip my shirt in sorrow
smear ashes on my breast,
dark promises oozing from my mouth.

I could shake with fear, never stop,
send anger ricocheting off the walls
as stomping boots kick dirt in day's dear face.

I could think 100 paths to vengeance.
Dark curses swarm, locusts
ravage rows of riot squads.

I could turn my fury loose
or pray for cleansing flames to break
the painted glass that blocks the Sun.

Summon Justice to our sides
and feed her lightning from our eyes.
Cry out her name in teeming streets.

Chant her into being this day.

20

Sunning easily, high on a wall
I dangle painted toes with pleasure
above noisy pushcarts in the streets below,
the flower sellers on the stairs.

Privilege is in the cells, not in the blood.
We eat its fruit and wear its gold,
born to lives we did not earn.
Our bodies made of stuff we stole.

These sweets so meanly bought
by sisters' blood and brothers' cries—
we tremble till we learn
to carry guilt and shoulder shame.

Use your voice and guide me now,
eyes on the stones and not the sky.
Into the streets where I will work
all night until forgiveness comes.

21

Now. This is when we pray.
When there is nothing left to do.
Then praying flows with every breath,
and we breathe each other's prayers.

Here. Wherever you are.
Go outside. Sigh for all of us.
Even if you do not know our names
let us ride the air with you.

There. Call out blessings
at each neighbor's gate,
chalk words of gratitude and wonder
to meet another prayer far down the road.

Open your mouth wide as the sky.
Your voice is louder than remembered.
Your reach is longer. Your mind wiser.
Your spirit always welcome.

22

Praise death's forgiveness.
As the loving gather
close to secrets,
her body's eyes are shut.

Did we not know,
as the last hour rose,
to close her fingers on our kisses,
blessings in her grasp?

Stay the night
with mother's stillness
confessing childish wishes
before she's turned to bliss.

We grieve, we count,
we cry for time,
fasten a wristwatch on the dead.

Please help me know what is enough,
and when time is of the essence.
Please turn Grandma's proverbs
into wisdom. It turns out,
I need it now.

So much to know.
A stitch in time—now or later?
A penny saved—which rainy day?
Beggars can't be choosers—
maybe we succumb to fate.

Don't count the chickens
before they're hatched.
And never put all my eggs
in one basket nor, hopelessly,
come up a day late and a dollar short.

Don't take any wooden nickels.
Or make a mountain out of a molehill.
Don't borrow trouble, and
promise never to throw the baby
out with the bathwater.

Don't cry over spilt milk, but
do strike while the iron is hot.
Because where there's a will,
there's a way, to let
the rising tide lift all boats.

Make hay while the sun shines
early enough to catch the worm.
Because any job worth doing is worth doing well.
See how many hands make light work
at home, where the heart is.

Bless me with what Grandma knew.
Tell me how she prayed.

24

Crushed velvet wraps
shoulders of earth's evening gown,
hills swoop into pocket canyons
deep enough for rain.
Show me.

Sleek black cows at pasture
scatter on the bodice,
French knots of fine embroidery
in a broken line across the heart.
Lift me.

Spring's first drapery
lining satin sleeves
with tufts of recollection
curling back on cuffs of tender scenes.
Join me.

Pulled up from underneath,
black thread twists
around the needle tip,
tacks the loop back down.
Watch me.

Mother's careful embroidery
in the small-town night
stitching linen napkins
for the woman she wanted to be.
Lift me.

Too soon she moves away.
A mossy sleeve against a lovely wrist,
fingertips lightly brush worn fence rails
descending near Time's stair.
Follow me. I will visit when I might.

25

I will keep my eyes open when I pray
to be ready for the light
which this day or another soon
will come to crack my hopeless heart.

I will listen for the sound of finches' wings
beating triplets in the air
arching up on branches lifted higher
than I ever imagined
I could reach.

26

Let me be a mourning dove's marmalade.
Let me be a knotting minuet of feathers.
Let me be footsteps whisking lightning under a chair.
Let me be linen covering iron bells in the cypress.
Let me be John Singer Sargent's Madam X as Madonna.
Let me be the opal eye of the Trumpet Swan.
Let me be Richard Serra's rusted curve
in Marguerite Duras' wasted arms.
Let me be a Calatrava crossing, one side to another.
Let me be a glass falcon in a sightless storm.
Let me be a crescent bowl of grace. Now.

27

Give me a day of Yes amongst gold crowns.
Sunflowers still lift themselves
in unabashed glory
unaware of milkweed silks blinking
across their sticky faces.

I promise I'll call to honeybees.
Let lady beetles ride my tilted face,
follow the daylong sky,
drop a thousand suns
into night on our horizon.

I'll nod with hundreds named to praise the sun.
Shoulders tremble. Prickly stems
stretch thready throats,
say *Yes* again.

I, too, look up.

Accept my plea. Teach me to bow.
Consecrate me to the Good.

28

When dusk turns to twilight,
find me on my knees,
humming *Hallelujah. Hallelujah!*

Leave the windows open to the inquiries of owls,
invite evening to exhale
daytime's noisy soul.

When night comes deep,
teach me to stop craving light
as darkness drops her wide-brimmed hat

like a new roof on the house I know.
Let us recognize each other
in silhouettes moving slow as fate

against the ecstatic horizon
of a painting by Rothko.
You know the one.

First, I'll have to get there
or better yet, here.

Reverence is easy,
even awe, for everything
that tingles in the rain.

Help me to lose myself
in the holiness of raindrops
feeding little starts of sugar peas
reaching up trellis strings
to become the hair of saints.

Tending sugar peas is easy.
Not so much the raindrops.
I understand the yearning tendrils
but not the calm of water
falling from the sky.

If I ask now, would you
take me inside the rain?
Or deny me and believe
that I've had awe enough, already.

30

Become a seeker, you say.
Look for what you might have lost,
left behind in the rush to pack
before the storm. The thunder
of distraction descends
to shake my shoulders,
lightning sets my eyelashes on fire.

How could I not wake
to your command?

Become a seeker, you say—
look for your Self.
Take the binoculars
from your ancestors,
look to the long view.
Scan the hills for footprints
to your soul's cave waiting.

Become a seeker, you say.
Look for your own true nature.
Yet every time I come near,
she scampers away and
pushes a little rowboat
out to sea.

31

Please take me someplace else.
Someplace other, someplace soft
where I might curl under wings
of comfort and blessed peace.

Shelter me from crowing hatred in the streets.
Take me away from tear gas clouds.
Allow me please to look away
and plan what next delight to eat.

I see you, Spirit, with your fist upraised
calling me to the rage of loss
to witness stories told by children
yet too weak to march.

Your Justice draws me tall,
pulls my voice from hiding,
calling out a new world,
one that we must make.

Summon a great rising
in our cities and our towns.
Build communion in the center
reaching out to tell your Truth.

Transform righteousness to Goodness,
infinite and shared. Let us
hold each other to our pledge
to wield our bold vast power.

32

Soothe my eyes with sky.
They ache with morning's arch
high across the rooftop.
Bound in bed, I listen
for the furtive feet of squirrels.

Show me the mountain.
Rising by her rocky self,
wildflowers stream below her breast,
flow to creeks,
catch her glory far from sight.

Lift me into treetops.
Lichen-ruffled branches
scratch at windows,
frame gusts of gingko leaves.

Allow me to forget myself.
Amidst the forests I cannot visit
and the shores I cannot wade,
I rise silent, ready to release the morning
to ants and honeysuckle, birdsongs and black bears.

33

What is hidden
does not belong to me.

What if it was stolen
from the forests and the fire?
What if it was pocketed
by the jays of morning? What
if I claimed someone else's joy?

Give it back, you say.
Your grandmother's baby bonnet
stitched by her auntie's maid.
Lost wages from the labor
of exhausted Black women
come by train from Georgia. Your
great-great grandfather's bank loan
on land your people could own.

Take it all, I say,
leave this one small hand
to scratch the dirt
by the porch stairs, sorting
lilac blossoms from gravel.

Let wind send the petals home.
Leave behind the stones for me,
smooth with kindness
or jagged with pain, saved
by generations before my time.

Teach me centuries in pebbles,
fill my pockets with the honor of nothing.

Crack me open. Do it now.

34

Friends, I fault myself for brokenness.
I have not stood still enough,
fallen to my knees enough,
prayed enough, to live
without relentless pain.

Anguish streams in blood tests
lost by long-dead doctors
who, amused by my beautiful ruin,
stylishly dressed in intelligence,
shrugged away my sorrow.

Friends, weave the winds into
a holy basket upturned for sanctuary,
gather to share breath
warm and well, under the dome
and into the center of being.

Lay me down amongst you
in the long peace of all directions,
close my eyes until
I lose myself to the heart of it,
my body finally lost to blessings.

Hear me pray. I give myself
to the Great Divines.
Herbs and horns and amulets
lay in a jumble as we kneel,
a nest of yearning made for chants.

Rebirth me slowly then,
twirl me wide-eyed,
a first embrace—
arms stretched wide enough
for a whole life.

35

What happens when I call
to you for love, or space, or comfort?
Call loud with need,
or whisper pleas, *sotto voce?*

Listen here. I'm calling you,
I know you hear. I see the sound
travel upwards on the wind
and roll behind the clouds.

You cannot disappear from me.
I will not be set aside,
I will talk back.
I'll make a scene.

My tantrums will wake
the children, will frighten
wolves with howls,
spit in your supper.

I've seen you shrug,
leave me to outwit pain
and surprise myself with
the cool blue smoke of gratitude.

When I give up, I beg you,
lie with me in a cradle of stardust.
Promise you won't leave me
cursed and hot with pain.

I will embroider
every leaf with your
one hundred names
set to shimmer in your light.

36

You called me to the far tip of the branch,
over tangled threads of moss.
I can barely balance there
in the waking dogwood blossoms.

Trembling with questions,
holding my breath,
I clutch the budding tip
and don't let go.

Morning Spirit, you give me
days written swiftly in pollen,
erased by your breath
before I can read them.

I crave your answers.
Will I live another year?
Who will set fire to my heart again?
Should I keep my eyes open, making love?

I want the answers all lined up,
starlings perched, shining, on a wire.
Some nod, *Yes.* Some, *No.*
None have all the answers.

Without questions, without answers,
look for me on the trembling limb
above the purple crocus bed,
holding onto the willow's first pale leaves.

37

The table is piled with gratitude
I did not summon but
which came with the chore:
photographs with flattened faces.
And bicycles.

Lakes and mountains and babies,
kept in labelled layers
from three dimensions to two,
as if they had been ironed
before they were laid down.

I pray to times forgotten,
linking lights behind the mist
crowding out the smiling
sunny day we found sand dollar
fossils on the beach.

Tell me, were they flat before
the Present ironed out scenes
of bivalve hinges turned to stone.
Tell me, please, how
to hold all time at once
or how to let it go.

38

I thought Grace would whisper,
shy and always kind.
I wait for murmurs bringing blessings to my room.

Then I hear pots banging in the street
tubas booming over shouts,
laughter, foot stomping.

I am waiting for Holiness,
I cry. *You woke me up.*

Good! the tuba player calls.
We've been trying for a week.

39

It is not I who has the loudest voice.

Let me be heard.

But no, you say.
Make yourself heard.
It's not my job to raise you up.

Don't pray for gifts
which you can give yourself.
You waste the tips of fingers
pressed together with this plea.

Ask me instead
for what is wild with brambles,
for the courage to make an altar
amongst the thorns.

40

Raise your arms,
bring sound up through hands,
vibrations living on skin.
I am tingling with time.

Call up the echoes.

Bennett's first cry, lifted out of me,
Don's perfect French, making up
nonsense words under a beret,
zeppelin windows whistling rush of sky,
hawks' wings beating over cypress trees,
Daddy singing *Ave Maria* while he cries.
There. Then.

Clanging bells of Venice,
deep gongs from San Marco,
dissonant knells from
Santa Maria Formosa and the Della Salute,
tumble into an ancient loft
at home in the Castello.
There. Then.

Costa Rica bullfrog chorus,
rain a tin roof clatter of slaps and claps,
my son shrieks in pain on the dining table,
a radio voice, calm, calls for surgery.
A tractor grunts through the mud
to pull us out, just before we sterilized the knife.
There. Then.

Insistent beats of salsa bands,
the rising moon a drumhead
tight with stars.
Drummers' fingers throb
with sexy promises after dark.
Congas call my lover to his past,
fling my spirit to the future.
There. Then.

The ancient singing bowl
rings out stories
set to quiver the pulse of now.

41

Every plea I make
is, as young Lord Byron wrote,
from the beginning to the end,
a selfish prayer for light.

I beg for stars to tumble
from the skies into
my upturned openness, eager
to gulp a spangled breath,

to fill me
when I'm nearly lost to dread,
crouched amongst holy things
strewn helter-skelter all around.

Call the others, please,
warn the multitude of goddesses
to pick up crosses here and shining scepters there,
flung off when we lost all hope and fled.

Let them tuck me in with sacred symbols,
crowd the crib with talismans,
rock me into sweetness
from anxious black despair.

Shake my morning head
gilded with their blessings
to set out once again
collecting wonder where I will.

42

Dear holy House,

You do not belong to me.
Anchored in your own sure self,
stone and story side-by-side
under the arbor of *cantera* saints.

Thank you for beauty,
trailing violet veils of bougainvillea
across a tangerine wall
cracked by yucca shadows.

Thank you for stillness,
the sighs of ancestors
lightly adrift through
windows left unlatched.

Thank you for lulling us to sleep,
for lacing up a cradle
of longed-for melodies
from the secret Before.

Your truth allows us our own time,
tender refuge without measure.
Now, full again, we leave you
to shelter others soon to come.

I offer you back to yourself
to summon those who need you next.

43

Roll the house on edge
till goodness runs to center.
We'll build an altar there
and ponder how to pray.

Call Kali, Joan of Arc, Tara and Kwan Yin.
Gather the sisters, mothers and saints.
Bring the Venus of Willendorf, Maria Dolorosa,
face upturned in anguished prayer.

Scoop up the Mighty Feminine.
Ring sacred bells to call the moon,
fill goblets full with incantations,
place candles at their feet.

Light the first and from that
light the others,
until we are all on fire with love.

44

Have you noticed?
I have come far
to sit beside you here,
eager, ready for grace.

I even practiced kneeling
by the bed, hands together,
a reverent child
praying for her mother.

I stole a dusty book, studied
Saint Francis, bowed and begging,
to learn just how to ask.

When the finger is cut,
or the heart broken,
when the roof flies with the wind,
or the century old sequoia
drops across the road,

does it interest
higher spirit minds
enough to interfere on earth?
Do you, Spirit, just keep playing
solitaire and shrug?

The morning breaks me open.
I've been waiting all night long
to walk barefoot by the lake,
dew on silver-painted toenails
dragging through the seagrass
where bullfrogs begged at dusk.

This place is holy all the time,
but I feel it most in morning,
at moonset when the Feminine
has just recharged the sky,
her silver fully spent
before the revelry of dawn.

I think the sun is Glory,
the moon Grace.
Fastened together with
knots of irrevocable vows,
sealed by unexpected Mercy
loosely braided with cold Fate.

Eagles plunge from white pine nests,
catch gleams of mirror fish
just out of reach,
loons in water temples
and baby muskrat kits,
blinking in the light.

Spirit, tell me,
Why is no one crying
at the beauty
and the burden?

46

Count me.

Call out my laziness.
Judge my selfishness.
Name indignities I did not see
and insults like blows
I never felt.

Count me.

Call me to justice,
to long due reparations
for looted lives. It is not
enough to add my prayers
to four centuries of pain.

Count me.

Take me out to other lives,
drop me to my knees
at the edge of a street
filled with lilies
and the wailing of sisters.

Count me.

Show me your fierce
faces, Priestesses,
fighting for your children's breaths
while our white history
suffocates their voices.

Count me.

I will listen to your stories.
I will witness your truth.
I will raise your banner.
I will stand beside you,
if it be your will.

47

Come, help me sleep.
Spirits, wrap me in the gauze
of Grandma's nightgown
here, under the attic eaves.

She lay her troubles down
to raise a yawning tent
of camphor calm
where I could hide to sleep.

To fall from barbed wire days
to oblivion under a crazy quilt
of Depression boarders' suits
left behind when they set out again.

Now nights gather thorns
in the bramble of darkness.
But I, tightrope walking
the thin light under the door,
refuse to jump into the sunrise.

48

Will you roll my body, like my spirit,
swaddle it with fierce protection
in blankets stitched with symbols
to ward off the bite of danger?

I've heard that Truth is naked,
bare, without threads of reason
from the rags of stories
made to entertain my lovers.

Skin lays wide open,
whatever you might make of it
without defense, without
a shroud to hide its wonder.

Unwrap the Truth of me.
Untie my ribbons of fear.
Let eagerness spill out.
Truth and generosity enough.

Tell me which it is.
Shoulders
of a much-embroidered coat.

49

Who prefers gold? who prefers blood?
Who prefers rice? who prefers beans?
Who prefers iron? who prefers feathers?
Who prefers sky? who prefers earth?
Who prefers running? who prefers walking?
Who prefers dogs? who prefers cats?
Who prefers the sun? who prefers the moon?

The Sisters, Night and Day,
are walking across the sky
shining down on the land.

Let us stand on the hills
to greet them.

Come. They are breathing out another day.
Another night. Another day.

50

I call you to wrap me in pink skies
marked by heaven-high redwoods
in their ancient season,
black against the dotted
golden trails of glowing tents.

We sit in your centuries under
the dusk-borne canopy of hope
your breath keeps aloft,
tied to the posts of a poet's lost rhyme.

I wait for you to lift me to the high arches
where cellos bow beams of light,
here I will learn your songs
for the phases of the moon.

I stretch my arms to you
full with the weight of evening
falling slowly over the woods
where my son used to hide.

I promise to bring your seed cones
to the altar. To invite forest mice
to breakfast there amidst
the sweetly fragrant boughs.

I promise not to forget.

51

Leaves drop,
the orange moon rises.
Children shake shiny eight-balls
for answers to their hopes.

Worried faces
peer at palms,
trace lines the Future drew
the day they were born.

Talismans hold up
the necks of holy women.
Some are crosses.
Most are not.

Myriad fetishes
perfumed by promise
line the coven's home
and populate the glow.

Mysteries dangle
golden charms above
the heads of seekers,
their heavy pockets full of fate.

We chase fear ahead of us
to hide behind the skirts of grace.
Call out fortune, beg the name
of what awaits us all.

A thousand fervent questions
drop from my mouth,
so eager to know more.
Body listening, I wait.
It is too soon to tell.

52

Help me leave my clothes
in a heap beside the bed
not to trouble kneeling
for this prayer, or any other.

Today, to stand still is enough.
Skin awakes to the stroke
of chimes from close cathedrals
and goatherds' bells on pastures far.

Restless vibrations of remembering
break me
wanting youth, adventurous and brave,
against the bed-bound crone.

Let my shoulders tingle with telling
the oldest stories
to your daughters.

Show me how we are the same.

ACKNOWLEDGMENTS

I have sought kinfolk in writers, artists, and musicians who were quiet renegades but whose voices carried both holy water and razor blades. Perhaps you and I have some of these in common.

I am thankful for Marcel Duchamp (Nude Descending a Staircase), Alexander Calder (Mercury Fountain), Joan Miro (invention of a visual language), El Greco (St. Francis), and Hiroshi Sugimoto (Seascapes) for teaching me to see with my heart.

The influence of these writers continues to shape me: Mirabai, Joan Didion, Marguerite Duras, Djuna Barnes, Doris Lessing, MFK Fisher, Lynn Freed, Marilyn Robinson, Grace Paley, Denise Levertov, Patti Smith, and Hafiz.

The musicians who kept me company while writing these poems are an eclectic mix: Laurie Anderson, John Luther Adams, Tord Gustavsen, Bill Evans, Joe Cocker, Jeff Beck, Jordi Savall, Bill Withers, Augustin Lara, James Blake, and Paco Pena.

The cluster of loved ones who sometimes make walls to protect me and sometimes invite me out to dance are the true blessings of my life: my husband, Don Kline; my son and daughter-in-law, Bennett and Diana Sell-Kline; my dearest friends Jenifer McKenna, Victoria Weiss, Martha Jessup, and Stephanie Berglund; and my siblings Steven, Michelle, and Lisette Sell.

For expert guidance from the skillful partners at my publisher, Wild Rising Press, Editor Judyth Hill and Book Designer Mary Meade, I offer enormous thanks.

And, of course, many more. With gratitude to all.

AUTHOR'S BIO

Collette Sell is a committed poet, gardener, and Buddhist practitioner. Each of these informs the others.

She is a member of the Marin Poetry Center, the O'Hanlon Center for the Arts, and San Miguel Pen. The San Miguel Writers' Conference and the San Miguel Literary Sala have deepened her commitment to craft. There she met poet Judyth Hill who continues to serve as both inspiration and editor for her work. Abby Wasserman's encouragement supported Collette as she found her voice, and The Grotto, an esteemed gathering place for writers in San Francisco, helped to open that voice. She has been published in *Tiferet: Offerings, Volume III* and *Pensive: A Global Journal of Spirituality & the Arts.*

Collette Sell has lived in one house for 39 years, and with one husband for 45 years. She doesn't move fast.

COLOPHON

Seeking a woman-designed font in a field historically
male-dominated, the author selected Kopius,
designed by Sibylle Hagmann,
an award-winning typeface designer.
Font *aficionados* describe Kopius as featuring
friendly characteristics suggesting brush strokes,
bestowing a texture-rich appearance,
and *having a warm yet serious demeanor.*
Kopius is a font complementary to
this gathering of prayers—
sent warmly to readers,
friend to friend... serving a deep, sweet purpose.

Made in the USA
Middletown, DE
10 April 2023

28483712R00050